TALK TO THE HOOF

Cartoons for People Who Love Horses

JARED LEE

RED PONY™
PRESS

JARED LEE STUDIO

This book is dedicated to my parents
who introduced their young sons
to the wonderful world of horses.

— JARED LEE

Printed in the United States of America

First Printing: January 2000
Second Printing: August 2000
Third Printing: April 2001
Fourth Printing: June 2002
Fifth Printing: October 2002
Sixth Printing: October 2003

Library of Congress Catalog Card Number 99-97818
ISBN 0-9677378-0-X

RED PONY™
P R E S S

A Division of Jared Lee Studio, Inc.

www.jaredlee.com

THE FARSIGHTED SHERIFF

HORSES KICK

wishful thinking

The Great Escape

THE DAWN of REASON

"Look, I said I was sorry for calling you Trigger."

SURGEON GENERAL'S WARNING:
Horses Are Addictive, Expensive,
And May Impair The Ability To
Use Common Sense.

JORED

School Horse

NO PAIN. NO SHAME.

"Doctor, I'd like to have this examined. I just bought ANOTHER HORSE!"

RIDING LESSON